LIFE'S HEALING CHOICES

GUIDED JOURNAL

FREEDOM FROM YOUR HURTS, HANG-UPS, *and* HABITS

HOWARD BOOKS
A DIVISION OF SIMON & SCHUSTER
New York   London   Toronto   Sydney

JOHN BAKER

Our purpose at Howard Books is to:

+ *Increase faith* in the hearts of growing Christians
+ *Inspire holiness* in the lives of believers
+ *Instill hope* in the hearts of struggling people everywhere

Because he's coming again!

Published by Howard Books, a division of Simon & Schuster, Inc.
1230 Avenue of the Americas, New York, NY 10020
www.howardpublishing.com

First Howard trade paperback edition September 2008

ISBN-13: 978-1-4165-5468-4
ISBN-10:   1-4165-5468-8

10   9   8   7   6   5   4   3   2   1

HOWARD and colophon are registered trademarks of Simon & Schuster, Inc.

Manufactured in the United States of America

For information regarding special discounts for bulk purchases, please contact: Simon & Schuster Special Sales at 1-800-456-6798 or business@simonandschuster.com.

Interior design by Masterpeace Studiology

Contents

How to Use
LIFE'S HEALING CHOICES
GUIDED JOURNAL

The purpose of the *Life's Healing Choices Guided Journal* is to provide you with a written account of your progress as you complete each of the eight Healing Choices found in the book, *Life's Healing Choices*. With each journal entry, you will be able to see, in black and white, the victories God is giving you over your hurts, hang-ups, and habits.

The *Life's Healing Choices Guided Journal* is divided into eight sections, one for each Healing Choice. Each section contains the "Make the Choice" segment found at the end of each chapter of *Life's Healing Choices*. You will be asked to answer several questions that will help guide you as you work on completing each Choice.

In addition, each of the eight sections contains several blank pages. As you journey through the eight Healing Choices, it is important to write down your thoughts, feelings, and insights. As God frees you from your hurts, hang-ups, and habits, He will reveal significant insights about yourself and others. On these pages, you can keep a daily journal of what God shows you and the progress and growth you are making day by day.

As you work though the *Life's Healing Choices Guided Journal* there will be days when you might fill a page. Other days you may only write a few sentences. That is up to you. The important thing is that you start a positive habit of writing in your journal every day. This will give you a written account of what God is doing in your life!

It is important to remember that our hurts, hang-ups, and habits did not occur overnight. Many of us have lived with our poor choices or the poor choices of others for years. We cannot expect to be free from them instantly.

On page 209 of the *Life's Healing Choices Guided Journal*, you will find the "Life's Healing Choices Prayer Journal." A prayer journal is simply writing down your prayer requests. Philippians 4:6–7 NIV tells us, "*Do not be anxious about anything, but in everything, by prayer and petition, with thanksgiving, present your requests to God. And the peace of God, which transcends all understanding, will guard your hearts and your minds in Christ Jesus.*"

The prayer journal pages are divided into two sections: "Prayer Request" and "God's Answer." It is exciting to look back and review your prayer journal and see how faithful God has been in answering your prayers. Just remember, God will answer your prayers according to His purpose and plan for your life. "*And my God will meet all your needs according to his glorious riches in Christ Jesus*" (Philippians 4:19 NIV).

Life's Healing Choices

Guided Journal

Realize I'm not God.

I *admit* that I am powerless to control
my tendency to do the wrong thing
and that my life is unmanageable.

R
E
C
O
V
E
R
Y

"Happy are those who know they are spiritually poor."
Matthew 5:3 TEV

Admitting NEED

Make the REALITY Choice

ACTION 1: *Pray about It*

Ask God to give you the courage to admit your inability to control yourself or your world. Pray that you will begin to depend on His power to help you make positive changes. Ask God to take control of your life and help you stop trying to control your image, other people, your problems, and your pain. Let Him know you are weary of carrying the fear, the frustration, the fatigue, and the failures of trying to be the general manager of the universe.

If you do not know all the words to pray and say to God right now, don't worry. You can pray as David did, *"God! Please hurry to my rescue! God, come quickly to my side!"* (Psalm 70:1 MSG).

Or you can pray:

Dear God, I want to take the first choice to healing and spiritual health today. I realize I am not You, God. I've often tried

3

to control my problems, my pain, my image, and even other people—as if I were You. I'm sorry. I've tried to deny my problems by staying busy and keeping myself distracted. But I'm not running anymore. I admit that I am helpless to control this tendency to do things I know are unhealthy for me. Today I am asking for Your help. I humbly ask You to take all the pieces of my unmanageable life and begin the process of healing. Please heal me. Please give me the strength to choose health. Help me stick with this process for the next seven choices. In Your name, I pray. Amen.

God will hear your cry for help and is ready to provide you with His strength, power, perfect love, and complete forgiveness as you choose to take your first step to healing!

After you prayed the REALITY CHOICE prayer, how do you feel? More important, what did God show you about yourself and your actions?

_____

_____

_____

_____

_____

_____

_____

ACTION 2: *Write about It*

The following questions will help you get started writing:

1. What people, places, or things do you have the power to control?

   _____

   _____

   _____

   _____

   _____

   _____

   _____

2. What people, places, or things have you been attempting to control? (Be specific.)

   _____

   _____

   _____

   _____

   _____

   _____

   _____

3. Describe how you try to control your image, other people, your problems, and your pain.

_____

_____

_____

_____

_____

_____

_____

4. Go back and read pages 18–20 of *Life's Healing Choices*. Write down how the fear, frustration, fatigue, and failures of trying to be the general manager of the universe has affected your relationships with God and others.

_____

_____

_____

_____

_____

_____

_____

5. What specific hurts, hang-ups, or habits have you been denying?

_____

_____

_____

_____

_____

_____

_____

You made it! Writing down the answers to these five questions was not easy, but it was a major beginning in your healing process. Now let's look at the third action.

ACTION 3: *Share about It*

As you move through the eight Healing Choices, you will discover that you need to share the life-changing truths God is showing you with someone you trust. The wise writer of Ecclesiastes said, *"Two are better than one, because they have a good return for their work: If one falls down, his friend can help him up. But pity the man who falls and has no one to help him up! . . . Though one may be overpowered, two can defend themselves. A cord of three strands is not quickly broken"* (Ecclesiastes 4:9–10, 12 NIV).

You are looking for someone you can talk to honestly and

openly. This person needs to be nonjudgmental and someone with whom you can safely share your personal journal notes. This person should be willing to share his or her life and struggles with you as well. Once God shows you that safe person, set up a meeting time and ask him or her to join with you in this recovery journey toward healing by being your accountability partner. This person may be a relative, a friend, a neighbor, a coworker, or someone in your church family.

Be sure the person you choose is of the same sex. You will be sharing very personal details of your life as you go through each of the Healing Choices. Some of the issues will be inappropriate to share with someone of the opposite sex.

If you cannot find a safe person to share with, visit www.celebraterecovery.com to locate a Celebrate Recovery group near you. There you will find people who have worked through the eight choices and who will be glad to help and support you as you begin your healing journey. Just remember, this journey should not be traveled alone. You need others to listen to you, encourage you, support you, and demonstrate God's love to you.

Write down the names of those individuals that you would consider sharing your Life's Healing Choices journey with.

_____

_____

_____

_____

_____

_____

_____

_____

Now write down why you think each of the people on your list would make a good accountability partner.

_____

_____

_____

_____

_____

_____

_____

_____

_____

After praying about the names on your list, who is your best choice?

_____

This is the person that you need to ask to be your accountability partner! Write out a plan of how you will ask that person to be your accountability partner.

_____

_____

_____

_____

NOTE: If the person you ask to be your accountability partner says no, do not take it personally. It may not be a good time for them or their own fears may cause them to decline. Whatever their reason, do not allow it to keep you from continuing your search. Simply ask another person on your list.

CHOICE 1

THE REALITY CHOICE
Realize I'm not God.

I admit that I am powerless to control my tendency to do the wrong thing and that my life is unmanageable.

As God frees you from your hurts, hang-ups, and habits, He will reveal significant insights about yourself and others. On these pages, you can keep a daily journal of what God shows you and the progress and growth you are making day by day.

"Happy are those who know they are spiritually poor."

MATTHEW 5:3 TEV

THE REALITY CHOICE
Realize I'm not God.

I admit that I am powerless to control
my tendency to do the wrong thing
and that my life is unmanageable.

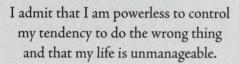

_____

_____

_____

_____

_____

_____

_____

_____

_____

_____

_____

_____

_____

_____

_____

_____

"There is a way that seems right to a man,
but in the end it leads to death."
Proverbs 14:12 NIV

"I don't understand myself at all, for I really want to do what is right, but I don't do it. Instead, I do the very thing I hate. I know perfectly well that what I am doing is wrong . . . but I can't help myself, because it is sin inside me that makes me do these evil things."

Romans 7:15–17 NLT

_____

_____

_____

_____

_____

_____

_____

_____

_____

_____

_____

_____

_____

_____

_____

_____

_____

_____

_____

_____

_____

_____

_____

_____

_____

_____

_____

_____

_____

CHOICE 1

THE REALITY CHOICE
Realize I'm not God.

I admit that I am powerless to control
my tendency to do the wrong thing
and that my life is unmanageable.

THE REALITY CHOICE
Realize I'm not God.

I admit that I am powerless to control
my tendency to do the wrong thing
and that my life is unmanageable.

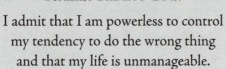

_____

_____

_____

_____

_____

_____

_____

_____

_____

_____

_____

_____

_____

_____

_____

_____

_____

_____

_____

_____

_____

_____

_____

_____

_____

_____

_____

_____

_____

_____

"Now I take limitations in stride, and with good cheer, these limitations that cut me down to size—abuse, accidents, opposition, bad breaks. I just let Christ take over! And so the weaker I get, the stronger I become."

2 Corinthians 12:10 MSG

"Two are better than one, because they have a good return for their work: If one falls down, his friend can help him up. But pity the man who falls and has no one to help him up!"

<small>ECCLESIASTES 4:9–10 NIV</small>

_____

_____

_____

_____

_____

_____

_____

_____

_____

_____

_____

_____

_____

_____

_____

_____

_____

_____

_____

_____

_____

_____

_____

_____

_____

_____

_____

_____

_____

CHOICE 1

THE REALITY CHOICE
Realize I'm not God.

I admit that I am powerless to control
my tendency to do the wrong thing
and that my life is unmanageable.

THE REALITY CHOICE
Realize I'm not God.

I admit that I am powerless to control
my tendency to do the wrong thing
and that my life is unmanageable.

_____

_____

_____

_____

_____

_____

_____

_____

_____

_____

_____

_____

_____

_____

_____

_____

_____

_____

_____

_____

_____

_____

_____

_____

_____

_____

_____

_____

_____

_____

_____

_____

_____

"He answered, 'I heard you in the garden, and
I was afraid because I was naked; so I hid.'"

Genesis 3:10 NIV

"It seems to be a fact of life that when I want to do what is right, I inevitably do what is wrong; . . . but there is something else deep within me . . . that is at war with my mind and wins the fight and makes me a slave to the sin that is still within me."

Romans 7:21, 23 TLB

_____

_____

_____

_____

_____

_____

_____

_____

_____

_____

_____

_____

_____

_____

_____

_____

_____

_____

_____

_____

_____

_____

_____

_____

_____

_____

_____

THE REALITY CHOICE
Realize I'm not God.

I admit that I am powerless to control
my tendency to do the wrong thing
and that my life is unmanageable.

THE REALITY Choice

Realize I'm not God.

I admit that I am powerless to control
my tendency to do the wrong thing
and that my life is unmanageable.

CHOICE 1

_____

_____

_____

_____

_____

_____

_____

_____

_____

_____

_____

_____

_____

_____

"There was a time when I wouldn't admit what a sinner I was. But my dishonesty made me miserable and filled my days with frustration."

PSALM 32:3 TLB

R

Earnestly believe that God exists,

that I *matter* to Him, and that He
has the power to help me recover.

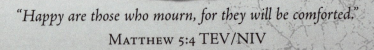

"Happy are those who mourn, for they will be comforted."
Matthew 5:4 TEV/NIV

C
O
V
E
R
Y

Getting HELP

Make the HOPE Choice

ACTION 1: *Pray about It*

Laying down your denial and trusting that God will give you the power may be a daily exercise for some time. But God's power is real and amazing. And day by day as we plug into that power, we will learn to trust Him more and more. Our job is to cry out for help and know He will keep His promise to hear our cries and help us.

Pray on your own, or read this prayer and pray these words in your heart:

Dear God, please help me not to ignore this pain You are using to alert me to my need for help. In the past, as I've ignored the denial busters You've allowed in my life, I have actually refused Your help. I am so sorry for this and ask Your help in facing the truth and trusting You to care for me. You know and care about all the pain and hurt I have in my life. Today I need Your help. I can't do it on my own. I have tried, and I keep coming up empty.

First, I pray for Your power in my life. I need Your power to break habits I can't break. I need Your power to help me do the things that I know are right but can't seem to do on my own. I need Your power to break free from my past. I ask for Your power to get on with the plans You have for my life.

Next, I pray for love. I want real love. I want to be able to love people and have them love me. I pray that with Your love I can let go of past hurts and failures so I can tear down the walls of fake intimacy. God, I ask You to help me have genuine intimacy with You and others. Help me to not be afraid of really loving and of really being loved.

I also pray for real self-control. I realize that I'm really not in control until I allow Christ to be in control of my life and circumstances.

God, please grant me Your power, love, and self-control. Help me to continue making healing choices. Amen.

If you prayed that prayer, you just took a very significant step! Don't worry about understanding the how-tos right now; we will look at those in Choice 3. Just know that you are on your way to getting help for when you hurt!

After you prayed the HOPE CHOICE prayer, how do you feel? More important, what did God show you about yourself and your actions?

_____

_____

_____

_____

_____

_____

_____

ACTION 2: *Write about It*

Before you begin, take a minute and reread what you wrote in Choice 1. Sometimes we are in such a hurry to grow, to progress, that we do not take time to reflect on what God has already taught us about Himself or ourselves. Your journal will give you an encouraging picture of your growth as you move through these eight choices.

With that said, let's review the following scripture and see what principles we can draw from it: "*When you go through deep waters and great trouble, I will be with you. When you go through rivers of difficulty, you will not drown! When you walk through the fire of oppression, you will not be burned up; the flames will not consume you*" (Isaiah 43:2 NLT).

God promises to be with you today, tomorrow, next week, next month, and next year as you face those issues you've been afraid to change all your life. Write out the answers to the following questions:

1. What pain has God been using as a megaphone in your life to alert you to your need for help?

_____

_____

_____

_____

_____

_____

_____

2. Who or what have you blamed for your problems—either partially or completely?

_____

_____

_____

_____

_____

_____

3. What pain have you been denying?

_____

_____

_____

_____

_____

_____

_____

4. What denial busters, found on pages 41–43 of *Life's Healing Choices* (crisis, confrontation, catastrophe), has God used to try to get your attention?

_____

_____

_____

_____

_____

_____

_____

_____

5. In what areas do you feel stuck in the pain of your past—powerless to change?

_____

_____

_____

_____

_____

_____

_____

_____

6. In what area(s) of your life are you now ready to allow God to start helping you?

_____

_____

_____

_____

_____

_____

_____

_____

7. What are you still afraid to turn over to God?

_____

_____

_____

_____

_____

_____

_____

_____

8. How are your feelings for your earthly father and heavenly
    Father alike? How do they differ?

_____

_____

_____

_____

_____

_____

_____

_____

ACTION 3: *Share about It*

This may be the most difficult of the three actions for you to take. But the good news is that it gets easier as you continue to go through each of the eight choices. God's Word says, *"As iron sharpens iron, so people can improve each other"* (Proverbs 27:17 NCV).

If you have already found someone to hold you accountable, write down how being able to share your hurts, hang-ups, and habits with another person has made you feel.

_____

_____

_____

_____

_____

If you are still looking for a safe person to share your healing journey with, writing down the answers to the following seven questions will help you in your search:

1. *Does he or she have a growing relationship with Jesus Christ?* **Do you see the character of Christ developing in this person?**

_____

_____

_____

2. *Does this person's walk and talk match?* Some Christians can quote the Bible, chapter and verse, but their lifestyle does not match their talk. Be certain that the person you choose to share your journey with is someone whose life is worthy of imitation.

_____

_____

_____

3. *Is he or she a good listener?* Do you sense that this person honestly cares about what you have to say?

_____

_____

_____

4. *Does he or she show compassion, concern, and hope but not pity?* You don't need someone to feel sorry for you, but you do need someone who can be sensitive to your pain.

_____

_____

_____

5. *Is this person strong enough to confront your denial or procrastination?* Does he or she care enough about you and your progress to challenge you? There is a difference

between helping others and trying to fix others. You need to be careful to guard the relationship from becoming unhealthy or codependent.

_____

_____

_____

6. *Does he or she offer suggestions?* Sometimes we need help in seeing options or alternatives that we are unable to find on our own.

_____

_____

_____

7. *Can this person share his or her own past and current struggles with you?* Is this person willing to open up and be vulnerable and transparent with you?

_____

_____

_____

The journey to a happy, healthy, whole life is not easy. Along the way, you will have to face some problems you have not wanted to deal with. You'll have to take some risks. This journey is not one to be traveled alone. You need someone of the same sex, a trusted friend, with whom you can share what God is doing in your life. As you complete this choice, focus on the hope found in God's love for you and His ability to help you heal.

CHOICE 2

THE HOPE CHOICE

Earnestly believe that God exists,

that I matter to Him, and that He has the power to help me recover.

As God frees you from your hurts, hang-ups, and habits, He will reveal significant insights about yourself and others. On these pages, you can keep a daily journal of what God shows you and the progress and growth you are making day by day.

THE HOPE CHOICE

Earnestly believe that God exists,

that I matter to Him, and that He
has the power to help me recover.

_____

_____

_____

_____

_____

_____

_____

_____

_____

_____

_____

_____

_____

_____

_____

_____

_____

_____

_____

_____

_____

_____

_____

_____

_____

_____

_____

_____

_____

_____

"Happy are those who mourn, for they will be comforted."
MATTHEW 5:4 TEV/NIV

"To all who mourn Israel, he will give beauty for ashes,
joy instead of mourning, praise instead of despair.
For the Lord has planted them like strong
and graceful oaks for his own glory"
ISAIAH 61:3 NLT

_____

_____

_____

_____

_____

_____

_____

_____

_____

_____

_____

_____

_____

_____

_____

_____

_____

_____

_____

_____

_____

_____

_____

_____

_____

_____

_____

The HOPE Choice

Earnestly believe that God exists,

that I matter to Him, and that He
has the power to help me recover.

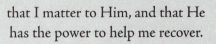

THE HOPE CHOICE

CHOICE 2

Earnestly believe that God exists,

that I matter to Him, and that He
has the power to help me recover.

_____

_____

_____

_____

_____

_____

_____

_____

_____

_____

_____

_____

_____

_____

_____

_____

_____

_____

_____

_____

_____

_____

_____

_____

_____

_____

_____

_____

_____

_____

_____

_____

_____

"Without faith it is impossible to please God, because anyone who comes to him must believe that he exists and that he rewards those who earnestly seek him."
HEBREWS 11:6 NIV

"I am radiant with joy because of your mercy, for you have listened to my troubles and have seen the crisis in my soul."

PSALM 31:7 TLB

_____

_____

_____

_____

_____

_____

_____

_____

_____

_____

_____

_____

_____

_____

_____

_____

_____

_____

_____

_____

_____

_____

_____

_____

_____

_____

_____

_____

_____

_____

_____

THE HOPE CHOICE

Earnestly believe that God exists,

that I matter to Him, and that He
has the power to help me recover.

CHOICE 2

45

THE HOPE CHOICE

Earnestly believe that God exists,

that I matter to Him, and that He
has the power to help me recover.

_____

_____

_____

_____

_____

_____

_____

_____

_____

_____

_____

_____

_____

_____

_____

_____

*"Do not be like them, for your Father knows
what you need before you ask him."*
MATTHEW 6:8 NIV

"The LORD is close to the brokenhearted and saves those who are crushed in spirit."

PSALM 34:18 NIV

_____

_____

_____

_____

_____

_____

_____

_____

_____

_____

_____

_____

_____

_____

_____

_____

_____

_____

_____

_____

_____

_____

_____

_____

_____

_____

_____

_____

_____

_____

CHOICE 2

THE HOPE CHOICE
Earnestly believe that God exists,
that I matter to Him, and that He
has the power to help me recover.

The HOPE Choice

Earnestly believe that God exists,

that I matter to Him, and that He
has the power to help me recover.

_____

_____

_____

_____

_____

_____

_____

_____

_____

_____

_____

_____

_____

_____

_____

_____

_____

_____

_____

_____

_____

_____

_____

_____

_____

_____

_____

_____

_____

_____

_____

_____

"You know how troubled I am; you have kept a record
of my tears. Aren't they listed in your book?"
Psalm 56:8 TEV

R

E

Consciously choose

O

to *commit* all my life and will
to Christ's care and control.

V

E

R

Y

"*Happy are the meek.*"
MATTHEW 5:5 TEV/NIV

Letting GO

Make the COMMITMENT Choice

ACTION 1: *Pray about It*

If you have not as yet asked Christ into your life—it's time to do so! You can start by rereading "Stepping Across the Line" on pages 81–83 of *Life's Healing Choices*. Then you can ask Christ into your life by praying this simple prayer:

Dear God, I believe You sent Your Son, Jesus, to die for my sins so I can be forgiven. I'm sorry for my sins, and I want to live the rest of my life the way You want me to. Please put Your Spirit in my life to direct me. Amen.

Congratulations! If you prayed that prayer for the first time, welcome to God's family! Please do not feel you need to understand everything about the commitment you just made. Understanding will come as you grow and mature in your walk with Christ. For now, let these words be your comfort: Jesus says,

"Are you tired? Worn out? Burned out on religion? Come to me. Get away with me and you'll recover your life. I'll show you how to take a real rest. Walk with me and work with me—watch how I do it. Learn the unforced rhythms of grace. I won't lay anything heavy or ill-fitting on you. Keep company with me and you'll learn to live freely and lightly" (Matthew 11:28–30 MSG).

There's more good news! "What this means is that those who become Christians become new persons. They are not the same anymore, for the old life is gone. A new life has begun!" (2 Corinthians 5:17 NLT). As you complete the remaining five choices, your life will never be the same. Your new life has begun!

If you have previously asked Christ into your heart, use this prayer time to commit to continually seek and follow His will for your life.

After you prayed the COMMITMENT CHOICE prayer, how do you feel? More important, what did God show you about yourself and your actions?

_____

_____

_____

_____

_____

_____

_____

ACTION 2: *Write about It*

Take some time to reflect on the commitment you just made—
whether it was your first commitment to Christ or a renewed
commitment to continually turn everything over to His care.
Committing to Christ is the most important decision you will ever
make. You will never be alone again. As you begin your journaling
for this choice, start off by answering the following questions,
which will help you organize your thoughts and emotions:

1. Go back to Choice 1, page 5 under "Action 2: Write about
    It." Reread your answers to questions 1 through 3. Write
    about how you feel differently about them today.

    _____

    _____

    _____

    _____

    _____

2. How do you feel, now that the burden of trying to control
    all the people, places, or things in your life has been lifted
    from you?

    _____

    _____

    _____

    _____

3. What does the following phrase mean to you? *"The old life is gone. A new life has begun!"* (2 Corinthians 5:17 NLT)

_____

_____

_____

_____

_____

_____

_____

4. What are some of the first things you will ask God to do in your new life?

_____

_____

_____

_____

_____

_____

_____

_____

5. What are you having a difficult time letting go of? What is stopping you from turning these things over to God's control?

_____

_____

_____

_____

_____

_____

_____

_____

ACTION 3: *Share about It*

It's important that you share your decision to ask Christ into your life with others. Follow God's direction found in His Word: *"If you confess with your mouth, 'Jesus is Lord,' and believe in your heart that God raised him from the dead, you will be saved"* (Romans 10:9 NIV). Each time you share your decision, it reconfirms your commitment. Your sharing also lets others know the reason for the freedom and joy you now have in your life.

Celebrate the Good News of your commitment with the person you have chosen to be your accountability partner. Let him or her know how you are feeling and what led you to turn the care and control of your life over to Christ. Be sure to share the things you are having a difficult time letting go of (your answer to question 5 on page 57).

Ask your accountability partner to pray with and for you. As you pray together, thank God for your willingness to make the onetime decision to ask Christ into your life as your Lord and Savior. Pray that you will daily choose to seek and follow God's will for your new life.

You've made it through the third choice. You are well on your way to a happier, healthier life—one lived in your Father's will, by His power and not your own.

Write down how you felt when you shared your commitment that you made in Choice 3.

_____

_____

_____

_____

_____

_____

_____

_____

_____

CHOICE 3

THE COMMITMENT CHOICE

Consciously choose to commit
all my life and will to Christ's care and control.

As God frees you from your hurts, hang-ups, and habits, He will reveal significant insights about yourself and others. On these pages, you can keep a daily journal of what God shows you and the progress and growth you are making day by day.

The COMMITMENT Choice

Consciously choose to commit

all my life and will to Christ's care and control.

_____

_____

_____

_____

_____

_____

_____

_____

_____

_____

_____

_____

_____

_____

_____

_____

_____

_____

_____

_____

_____

_____

_____

_____

_____

_____

_____

_____

_____

_____

_____

"Happy are the meek."
MATTHEW 5:5 TEV/NIV

"No one is respected unless he is humble;
arrogant people are on the way to ruin."
PROVERBS 18:12 TEV

_____

_____

_____

_____

_____

_____

_____

_____

_____

_____

_____

_____

_____

_____

CHOICE 3

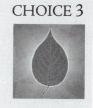

The COMMITMENT Choice

Consciously choose to commit

all my life and will to Christ's care and control.

The COMMITMENT Choice

Consciously choose to commit

all my life and will to Christ's care and control.

_____

_____

_____

_____

_____

_____

_____

_____

_____

_____

_____

_____

_____

_____

_____

_____

_____

_____

_____

_____

_____

_____

_____

_____

_____

_____

_____

_____

_____

_____

*"The wise man is glad to be instructed, but
a self-sufficient fool falls flat on his face."*
PROVERBS 10:8 TLB

*"I have swept away your sins like the morning mists. I have scattered
your offenses like the clouds. Oh, return to me, for I
have paid the price to set you free."*

ISAIAH 44:22 NLT

_____

_____

_____

_____

_____

_____

_____

_____

_____

_____

_____

_____

_____

_____

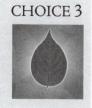

CHOICE 3

The COMMITMENT Choice

Consciously choose to commit

all my life and will to Christ's care and control.

THE COMMITMENT CHOICE

Consciously choose to commit

all my life and will to Christ's care and control.

_____

_____

_____

_____

_____

_____

_____

_____

_____

_____

_____

_____

_____

_____

_____

_____

_____

_____

_____

_____

_____

_____

_____

_____

_____

_____

_____

_____

_____

"I am sure that God who began the good work within you will keep
right on helping you grow in his grace until his task within you is
finally finished on that day when Jesus Christ returns."
Philippians 1:6 TLB

"My God, I want to do what you want. Your teachings are in my heart."
PSALM 40:8 NCV

_____

_____

_____

_____

_____

_____

_____

_____

_____

_____

_____

_____

_____

_____

_____

_____

_____

_____

_____

_____

_____

_____

_____

_____

_____

_____

_____

_____

_____

_____

_____

The COMMITMENT Choice

Consciously choose to commit

all my life and will to Christ's care and control.

CHOICE 3

THE COMMITMENT CHOICE

Consciously choose to commit

all my life and will to Christ's care and control.

_____

_____

_____

_____

_____

_____

_____

_____

_____

_____

_____

_____

_____

_____

_____

_____

_____

_____

_____

_____

_____

_____

_____

_____

_____

_____

_____

_____

_____

_____

_____

_____

_____

_____

_____

"I can do everything God asks me to with the help
of Christ who gives me the strength and power."
Philippians 4:13 TLB

R
E
C

Openly examine

V

and *confess* my faults to myself,

to God, and to someone I trust.

E

R

Y

"Happy are the pure in heart."
MATTHEW 5:8 TEV

Coming
CLEAN

Make the HOUSECLEANING Choice

ACTION 1: *Pray about It*

Facing your past and being honest about your guilt is not easy. You need God's help to take each step in this choice. Prayer is the best way to tap into His power. You can pray your own words or use these . . .

Dear God, You know my past—all the good and bad choices I have made and all the good and bad things I have done. In working through Choice 4, I ask that You give me the strength and courage to list the items called for in the "Write about It" section below so that I can come clean and face the truth. Please open my eyes to the truth of my past—the truth of how others have hurt me and how I have hurt others. Please help me reach out to others You have placed along my pathway to healing. Thank You for providing these individuals to help me keep balanced as I do my inventory.

As I come clean in this choice, I thank You in advance for the forgiveness You have given me. In Christ's name I pray. Amen.

After you prayed the HOUSECLEANING CHOICE prayer, how do you feel? More important, what did God show you about yourself and your actions?

_____

_____

_____

_____

_____

ACTION 2: *Write about It*

Take a minute to review what you wrote in Choices 1–3 in the "Write about It" sections. It's important that you complete each chapter to the best of your ability before moving on to the next. The Bible encourages us in our efforts: *"Let us examine our ways and test them, and let us return to the LORD"* (Lamentations 3:40 NIV).

On the following pages, you will have an opportunity to start working on your Moral Inventory. Go back and reread pages 106–14 of *Life's Healing Choices*. On pages 78–81, you will find a chart with five sections for you to complete. They are:

1: *The Person*—In this section, list the person or object you resent or fear. Go as far back as you can. Remember that resentment is mostly unexpressed anger, hurt, or fear.

2: *The Cause*—It has been said that "hurt people hurt people." In this section, list the specific actions someone did to hurt you.

3: *The Effect*—In this section write down how that specific, hurtful action affected your life both in the past and in the present.

4: *The Damage*—In this section write down which of your basic needs were injured. *Social*—Have you suffered from broken relationships, slander, or gossip? *Security*—Has your physical safety been threatened? Have you faced financial loss? *Sexual*— Have you been a victim in abusive relationships? Has intimacy or trust been damaged or broken?

5: *My Part*—In this section you need to honestly determine and write down the part of the resentment or any other sin or injury that you are responsible for. Ask God to show you your part in a broken or damaged marriage or relationship, a distant child or parent, or maybe a job loss. List the people you have hurt and how you specifically hurt them.

PLEASE NOTE: If you have been in an abusive relationship, especially as a small child, you can find great freedom in this part of the inventory. You will see that you had *no* part, *no* responsibility, for the cause of the resentment. By simply writing the words "NONE" or "NOT GUILTY" in section 5, you can begin to be free from the misplaced shame and guilt you have carried with you.

You may need to use additional sheets of paper to complete your moral inventory.

*"Let us examine our ways and test them, and let us
return to the Lord."* LAMENTATIONS 3:40 NIV

---

1. The Person

_____

_____

_____

---

2. The Cause

_____

_____

_____

---

3. The Effect

_____

_____

_____

---

4. The Damage

_____

_____

_____

---

5. My Part

_____

_____

_____

*"Let us examine our ways and test them, and let us
return to the Lord."* LAMENTATIONS 3:40 NIV

---

1. The Person

---

2. The Cause

---

3. The Effect

---

4. The Damage

---

5. My Part

*"Let us examine our ways and test them, and let us
return to the Lord."* LAMENTATIONS 3:40 NIV

1. The Person _____

_____

_____

2. The Cause _____

_____

_____

3. The Effect _____

_____

_____

4. The Damage _____

_____

_____

5. My Part _____

_____

_____

"Let us examine our ways and test them, and let us return to the Lord." LAMENTATIONS 3:40 NIV

---

1. The Person

---

2. The Cause

---

3. The Effect

---

4. The Damage

---

5. My Part

ACTION 3: *Share about It*

In your "Write about It" action step, you spent some serious time listing some difficult truths. Now it's time to share those truths aloud with your trusted friend. In your next meeting, go through your five sections and share it all. This is the second part of Choice 4—that you "openly confess your faults to someone you trust."

Take your time and have the courage to go through each section in your list:

- *The Person*—the one or ones you resent or fear

- *The Cause*—the reason you hurt

- *The Effect*—both past and present effects of the hurt

- *The Damage*—how you were hurt (socially, sexually, or made to feel insecure)

- *My Part*—here you take ownership for your role in the problem, large or small

Remember, saying the words aloud untangles the thoughts in your head, giving them shape and enabling you to face them productively. After you've shared these five topics, take a minute with your friend to thank God for His full forgiveness.

SPECIAL NOTE: Be careful to safeguard your inventory; this list is no one's business but yours, God's, and the special person you choose to share it with.

Describe the freedom you felt after you shared your Moral Inventory with your accountability partner.

_____

_____

_____

_____

_____

_____

_____

How do you think that finally being able to share the truth about your life with another will help you as you continue to complete the remaining four choices?

_____

_____

_____

_____

_____

_____

_____

THE HOUSECLEANING CHOICE

Openly examine and confess my faults

to myself, to God, and to someone I trust.

As God frees you from your hurts, hang-ups, and habits, He will reveal significant insights about yourself and others. On these pages, you can keep a daily journal of what God shows you and the progress and growth you are making day by day.

"Happy are the pure in heart."

MATTHEW 5:8 TEV

_____

_____

_____

_____

_____

_____

_____

_____

_____

_____

_____

_____

_____

_____

_____

_____

_____

_____

CHOICE 4

The HOUSECLEANING Choice
Openly examine and confess my faults
to myself, to God, and to someone I trust.

_____

_____

_____

_____

_____

_____

_____

_____

_____

_____

_____

_____

_____

_____

_____

_____

"What happiness for those whose guilt has been forgiven! What joys when sins are covered over! What relief for those who have confessed their sins and God has cleared their record."

PSALM 32:1–2 TLB

"Search me, O God, and know my heart; test my thoughts.
Point out anything you find in me that makes
you sad, and lead me along the path of everlasting life."
PSALM 139:23–24 TLB

_____

_____

_____

_____

_____

_____

_____

_____

_____

_____

_____

_____

_____

_____

_____

_____

_____

_____

_____

_____

_____

_____

_____

_____

_____

_____

_____

_____

CHOICE 4

THE HOUSECLEANING CHOICE

Openly examine and confess my faults

to myself, to God, and to someone I trust.

CHOICE 4

The HOUSECLEANING Choice

Openly examine and confess my faults

to myself, to God, and to someone I trust.

_____

_____

_____

_____

_____

_____

_____

_____

_____

_____

_____

_____

_____

_____

_____

_____

_____

_____

_____

_____

_____

_____

_____

_____

_____

_____

_____

_____

_____

_____

"The Lord gave us mind and conscience;
we cannot hide from ourselves."

Proverbs 20:27 TEV

*"If we claim to be without sin, we deceive
ourselves and the truth is not in us."*

1 John 1:8 NIV

_____

_____

_____

_____

_____

_____

_____

_____

_____

_____

_____

_____

CHOICE 4

The HOUSECLEANING Choice

Openly examine and confess my faults

to myself, to God, and to someone I trust.

The HOUSECLEANING Choice

Openly examine and confess my faults

to myself, to God, and to someone I trust.

\
\
\
\
\
\
\
\
\
\
\
\
\
\
\
\
\
\
\
\

_____

_____

_____

_____

_____

_____

_____

_____

_____

_____

_____

_____

_____

"Come, let's talk this over! says the Lord; no matter how deep the stain of
your sins, I can take it out and make you as clean as freshly fallen snow.
Even if you are stained as red as crimson, I can make you white as wool!"

Isaiah 1:18 TLB

"Admit your faults to one another and pray for each other so that you may be healed. The earnest prayer of a righteous man has great power and wonderful results."

JAMES 5:16 TLB

_____

_____

_____

_____

_____

_____

_____

_____

_____

_____

_____

_____

_____

_____

_____

_____

_____

_____

_____

_____

_____

_____

_____

_____

_____

_____

_____

_____

CHOICE 4

THE HOUSECLEANING CHOICE

Openly examine and confess my faults

to myself, to God, and to someone I trust.

THE HOUSECLEANING CHOICE

Openly examine and confess my faults

to myself, to God, and to someone I trust.

_____

_____

_____

_____

_____

_____

_____

_____

_____

_____

_____

_____

_____

_____

_____

_____

_____

_____

_____

_____

_____

_____

_____

_____

_____

_____

_____

_____

*"After you have suffered a little while, our God, who is full
of kindness through Christ, will give you his eternal glory.
He personally will come and pick you up, and set you firmly
in place, and make you stronger than ever."*

1 PETER 5:10 TLB

R
E
C
O

Voluntarily submit

E

to every *change* God wants to make

in my life and humbly ask Him

R

to remove my character defects.

Y

"Happy are those whose greatest desire is to do what God requires."

MATTHEW 5:6 TEV

Making CHANGES

Make the TRANSFORMATION Choice

ACTION 1: *Pray about It*

In chapter 5 of *Life's Healing Choices*, we talk a lot about character defects—where they come from, why it takes so long to get rid of them, and how we can cooperate with God to change them. You may be feeling a bit overwhelmed, so let's just pause and take a breath. We're not trying to fix everything at once. Remember the question, "How do you eat an elephant?" You do it one bite at a time. That's how you'll face your character defects—one defect at a time. So in this action step, we're going to put into practice one of the seven ways to cooperate with God. On page 137 of *Life's Healing Choices*, the first focus step listed is "Focus on changing one defect at a time." Look back at the moral inventory list you made on pages 78–81 of your journal. Through prayer, ask God to help you review this list and choose a place to start dealing with your defects of character. You can pray, using your own words or follow along with the prayer below:

Dear God, thank You for Your forgiveness. Now I am ready and willing to submit to any and all changes You want to make in my life. By Your grace, I am ready to face it and deal with the defects one by one.

I have defects that have hurt me and defects that have hurt others. I've lived with some of these defects for so long that they have become a part of who I am. I have tried by my own power to fight against my defects and have failed over and over. I now ask that by Your power and the power of Your Holy Spirit that You transform my mind, my heart, and my actions.

I need Your help in knowing where to start. I cannot handle all my defects at once. I can only face them one at a time. Show me, Lord, where should I begin? Help me as I look over my inventory list. Which character defect is the most damaging to my life? Where do I need to start? I am ready to follow Your lead. Amen.

After you have prayed the TRANSFORMATION CHOICE prayer, how do you feel? More important, what did God show you about yourself and your actions?

_____

_____

_____

_____

ACTION 2: *Write about It*

In addition to writing in your journal, this action step will provide you with some Bible promises to help you focus on the *good* things, not only the *bad*.

To begin, you'll need several 3x5 index cards. On one side of the card, write a positive Scripture verse. On the other side, write a practical application of the verse in the form of a personal affirmation. Here's an example.

On side one, write:

There is no condemnation for those who belong to Christ Jesus.
(Romans 8:1 NLT)

Turn it over and write:

God does not condemn me for my
_____. He loves me just as much on my bad days as on my good days. I can make it through today without _____ because Christ gives me His strength.

Here's another example.

Side one:

> Where God's love is,
> there is no fear,
> because God's perfect love
> drives out fear . . .
> (1 John 4:18 NCV)

Side two:

> Today is going to be a better day than yesterday, because God is helping me get stronger. Yesterday, I was worried about _____. Today, I'm not afraid because God loves me!

Some other verses you might use are:

+ *If anyone belongs to Christ, there is a new creation. The old things have gone; everything is made new!* (2 Corinthians 5:17 NCV)

+ *Those who know your name will trust in you, for you, Lord, have never forsaken those who seek you.* (Psalm 9:10 NIV)

+ *Trust in the LORD with all your heart and lean not on your own understanding; in all your ways acknowledge him, and he will make your paths straight.* (Proverbs 3:5–6 NIV)

+ *Commit to the* LORD *whatever you do, and your plans will succeed.* (Proverbs 16:3 NIV)

+ *Come to me, all of you who are tired and have heavy loads, and I will give you rest.* (Matthew 11:28 NCV)

+ *Do not worry about anything, but pray and ask God for everything you need, always giving thanks. And God's peace, which is so great we cannot understand it, will keep your hearts and minds in Christ Jesus.* (Philippians 4:6–7 NCV)

+ *Without faith no one can please God. Anyone who comes to God must believe that he is real and that he rewards those who truly want to find him.* (Hebrews 11:6 NCV)

Write out a whole stack of these. Every night when you go to bed, read the verses and affirmations and think about them. When you wake up in the morning before you get out of bed, read them again. Put them in your pocket or purse and read them throughout the day. As you think positive thoughts, your autopilot will be reprogrammed and new positive ruts will be created in your mind. In about four to five weeks, you will begin to notice a difference in how you feel.

Let's get started! Now that you have honestly faced the truth about your past, what is the defect God has guided you to focus on first? Why did you choose this one?

_____

_____

_____

_____

_____

Daily, as you write in your journal (on the blank pages) . . .

+ Keep a record of how journaling helps to change the way you feel about God, yourself, and others.

+ Write about the defect God has guided you to focus on first. Then record the progress (and setbacks) you are experiencing as you cooperate with God to focus on changing this one defect.

+ Spend time journaling about your efforts to "focus on _doing_ good, not _feeling_ good." It helps to write down the daily struggles and victories you have as you try to do the right thing, even when you don't feel like it.

As the weeks pass, you will see in black and white how you are overcoming certain defects of character. You will also begin to see other defects that you and God still need to work on. Having it all written down helps as you share your progress with your accountability partner.

ACTION 3: _Share about It_

If you shared your moral inventory list (your hurts, hang-ups, and habits) with your accountability partner, you've taken a big step in this sharing relationship. **If you haven't shared it yet, you need to do so before you go any further.** It is important to complete one choice completely, to the best of your ability, before moving on to the next. This is especially true with sharing your moral inventory. Your accountability partner can't help you work on your defects of character if he or she does not have all your information.

If you have shared your moral inventory, then you are ready to:

+ Share the one defect God has guided you to focus on changing first. Be honest about the character defect, how it has hurt you, and how it has hurt others.

+ Share the progress God is making in your life in changing this defect. Be honest about your level of cooperation.

+ Share about your efforts to act yourself into a better way of feeling. Share the negative feelings you're trying to replace, and share the positive actions you're taking even if you don't yet have the feelings to match.

Remember the promise in Proverbs, "*As iron sharpens iron, so one man sharpens another*" (Proverbs 27:17 NIV).

How did you feel after you shared the first defect of character that you want you and God to work on with your accountability partner?

_____

_____

_____

_____

_____

_____

What was his/her response?

_____

_____

_____

_____

_____

THE TRANSFORMATION CHOICE

Voluntarily submit to every change
God wants to make in my life and humbly
ask Him to remove my character defects.

As God frees you from your hurts, hang-ups, and habits, He will reveal significant insights about yourself and others. On these pages, you can keep a daily journal of what God shows you and the progress and growth you are making day by day.

The TRANSFORMATION Choice

Voluntarily submit to every change

God wants to make in my life and humbly
ask Him to remove my character defects.

_____

_____

_____

_____

_____

_____

_____

_____

_____

_____

_____

_____

_____

_____

_____

_____

_____

_____

_____

_____

_____

_____

_____

_____

_____

_____

_____

_____

_____

_____

_____

_____

"Happy are those whose greatest desire is to do what God requires."
Matthew 5:6 TEV

*"Offer yourselves as a living sacrifice to God,
dedicated to his service and pleasing to him. . . . Let God transform
you inwardly by a complete change of your mind."*
Romans 12:1–2 TEV

_____

_____

_____

_____

_____

_____

_____

_____

_____

_____

_____

_____

_____

_____

_____

_____

_____

_____

_____

_____

_____

_____

_____

_____

_____

_____

_____

_____

_____

_____

_____

THE TRANSFORMATION CHOICE

Voluntarily submit to every change

God wants to make in my life and humbly
ask Him to remove my character defects.

The TRANSFORMATION Choice

Voluntarily submit to every change

God wants to make in my life and humbly
ask Him to remove my character defects.

_____

_____

_____

_____

_____

_____

_____

_____

_____

_____

_____

_____

_____

_____

_____

_____

_____

_____

_____

_____

_____

_____

_____

_____

_____

_____

_____

_____

_____

"Stay alert, be in prayer, so you don't enter the danger zone
without even knowing it. Don't be naive. Part of you is eager,
ready for anything in God; but another part is as lazy
as an old dog sleeping by the fire."

Mark 14:38 MSG

"You will know the truth, and the truth will set you free."

John 8:32 NIV

_____

_____

_____

_____

_____

_____

_____

_____

_____

_____

_____

_____

_____

_____

_____

_____

_____

_____

_____

_____

_____

_____

_____

_____

_____

_____

_____

_____

_____

_____

CHOICE 5

THE TRANSFORMATION CHOICE

Voluntarily submit to every change

God wants to make in my life and humbly
ask Him to remove my character defects.

CHOICE 5

The TRANSFORMATION Choice

Voluntarily submit to every change

God wants to make in my life and humbly
ask Him to remove my character defects.

_____

_____

_____

_____

_____

_____

_____

_____

_____

_____

_____

_____

"Fix your thoughts on what is true and good and right. Think about things that are pure and lovely, and dwell on the fine, good things in others. Think about all you can praise God for and be glad about."
PHILIPPIANS 4:8 TLB

"Do not be fooled: 'Bad friends will ruin good habits.'"

1 Corinthians 15:33 NCV

_____

_____

_____

_____

_____

_____

_____

_____

_____

_____

_____

_____

_____

_____

_____

_____

_____

_____

_____

_____

_____

_____

_____

_____

_____

_____

_____

_____

_____

_____

_____

_____

_____

_____

THE TRANSFORMATION CHOICE

Voluntarily submit to every change

God wants to make in my life and humbly
ask Him to remove my character defects.

The TRANSFORMATION Choice

Voluntarily submit to every change

God wants to make in my life and humbly
ask Him to remove my character defects.

_____

_____

_____

_____

_____

_____

_____

_____

_____

_____

_____

_____

_____

_____

_____

_____

_____

_____

_____

_____

_____

_____

_____

_____

_____

_____

_____

_____

_____

_____

_____

_____

_____

"As iron sharpens iron, so one man sharpens another."
PROVERBS 27:17 NIV

R
E
C
O
V
E
R
Y

Evaluate all my relationships.

Offer *forgiveness* to those who have hurt me,
and make amends for harm I've done to others,
except when to do so would harm them or others.

"*Happy are those who are merciful to others.*"
MATTHEW 5:7 TEV

"*Happy are those who work for peace.*"
MATTHEW 5:9 TEV

Repairing RELATIONSHIPS

Make the RELATIONSHIP Choice

ACTION 1: *Pray about It*

You've worked through the first five choices; you've made a lot of progress toward becoming the healthy, whole individual God created you to be. The two-part process in this choice will bring you even closer to your goal, for in it you will find the healing of relationships—for broken relationships lie at the root of so much of our pain. But the choices cannot be made alone. You need God's help to follow through. In this action step, we will ask God to help us both forgive those who have hurt us and make amends to those whom we have hurt. The freedom and hope found at the end of this process will bring you great release. Use your own words to ask God's help, or join in the prayer below:

Dear God, You have shown me that holding on to resentment for the wrongs done to me and refusing to make right my own wrongs has crippled me—emotionally, spiritually, and even physically. I ask You today to help me be honest about the hurts I feel. I've stuffed some and ignored others, but now I am ready to come clean and tell the truth about my pain. As I do, I ask that You give me the strength and the courage so I can release those who have hurt me and let go of my resentment toward them. Only by Your power will I be able to do this, Lord.

I pray, also, that You will give me the courage and discernment to know how to make amends to those I have hurt. Help me to be honest as I look back and remember, and guide me as I find the ways to make restitution, where appropriate.

Finally, I pray that I can begin a new life today as I refocus my life on doing Your will in my relationships. Help me set aside my selfishness and set my whole heart on You—I know I have a long way to go. I want the promise found in Job that all my troubles will fade from my memory and be remembered no more. Amen.

After you prayed the RELATIONSHIP CHOICE prayer, how do you feel? More important, what did God show you about yourself and your actions?

_____

_____

_____

_____

ACTION 2: *Write about It*

Now is the time to get some important issues down in black and white.

Those You Need to Forgive

We'll begin by dealing with those who have hurt you—those you need to forgive. Remember, admitting that someone has hurt you and that you are angry about what he or she has done does not mean you don't love this person. You can be angry with a person whom you love very much.

Here's how you begin: You make a list of those who have harmed you. Go back and review once more the names you wrote down in your Moral Inventory in Choice 4, section "The Person," on pages 78–81 of your journal.

Write down:

+ his or her name and relationship to you

+ what this person said that hurt you

+ what he or she did that hurt you

+ how the hurt made you feel

Write it all down on your "Forgiveness List," starting on the following page, so you can look at it. You may need additional sheets of paper to complete your Forgiveness List. When you write things down, they lose their fuzzy quality and become real. Think about that teacher who embarrassed you or the parent who said, "You'll never amount to anything; you're a failure." That former boyfriend/girlfriend/husband/wife/friend who was unfaithful to you. The person who abused you as a child. Write it all down, and reveal your hurt. This is your Forgiveness List:

LIFE'S
Healing Choices
FORGIVENESS LIST

1. His or her name and relationship to you. _____

_____

_____

_____

2. What this person said that hurt you. _____

_____

_____

_____

3. What he or she did that hurt you. _____

_____

_____

_____

4. How the hurt made you feel. _____

_____

_____

_____

LIFE'S
Healing Choices
FORGIVENESS LIST

1. *His or her name and relationship to you.* _____

_____

_____

_____

2. *What this person said that hurt you.* _____

_____

_____

_____

3. *What he or she did that hurt you.* _____

_____

_____

_____

4. *How the hurt made you feel.* _____

_____

_____

_____

LIFE'S *Healing Choices* FORGIVENESS LIST

1. *His or her name and relationship to you.*_____

_____

_____

_____

2. *What this person said that hurt you.* _____

_____

_____

_____

3. *What he or she did that hurt you.* _____

_____

_____

_____

4. *How the hurt made you feel.* _____

_____

_____

_____

LIFE'S
Healing Choices
FORGIVENESS LIST

1. *His or her name and relationship to you.*

_____

_____

_____

2. *What this person said that hurt you.*

_____

_____

_____

3. *What he or she did that hurt you.*

_____

_____

_____

4. *How the hurt made you feel.*

_____

_____

_____

Those to Whom You Need to Make Amends

You made your Forgiveness List of those who have harmed you. Now you need to make an "Amends List" of those you have harmed. Write down:

- his or her name and relationship to you

- what you said to hurt this person

- what you did to hurt him or her

- how you think you made this person feel

- why you are sorry for hurting him or her

Once again, when you write it down in your Amends List and get it down in black and white, the offense becomes real. It is no longer vague: "I think I may have hurt her with my words when I was angry." When you write it out, it becomes, "This is how I hurt her with my words when I lost my temper that night." Your Amends List makes your responsibility specific. Go back and review once more the names you wrote down in the Moral Inventory in Choice 4, section 5, "My Part," on pages 78–81 of your journal.

If you are having trouble thinking of anybody you have hurt, perhaps these questions will get you started:

- Is there anyone to whom you owe a debt that you haven't repaid? A friend, a family member, a business?

+ Is there anyone you've broken a promise to? A parent, a spouse, a child?

+ Is there anyone you are guilty of controlling or manipulating? A spouse, a child, a brother, an employee, a friend?

+ Is there anyone you are overly possessive of? A spouse, a child, a coworker?

+ Is there anyone you are hypercritical of? A spouse, a child?

+ Have you been verbally, emotionally, or physically abusive to anyone?

+ Is there anyone you have not appreciated or paid attention to?

+ Did you forget a child's birthday or your anniversary?

+ Is there anyone you have been unfaithful to?

+ Have you ever lied to anyone?

That's enough to get you started. If you still do not have anyone on your list, go back to Choice 1 and start all over again! You may need additional sheets of paper to complete your Amends List.

LIFE'S
Healing Choices
AMENDS LIST

1. *His or her name and relationship to you.*

_____

_____

2. *What you said to hurt this person.*

_____

_____

3. *What you did to hurt him or her.*

_____

_____

4. *How you think you made this person feel.*

_____

_____

5. *Why you are sorry for hurting him or her.*

_____

_____

_____

LIFE'S
Healing Choices
AMENDS LIST

1. *His or her name and relationship to you.* _____

_____

_____

2. *What you said to hurt this person.* _____

_____

_____

3. *What you did to hurt him or her.* _____

_____

_____

4. *How you think you made this person feel.* _____

_____

_____

5. *Why you are sorry for hurting him or her.* _____

_____

_____

_____

LIFE'S
Healing Choices
AMENDS LIST

1. *His or her name and relationship to you.*_____

_____

_____

2. *What you said to hurt this person.*_____

_____

_____

3. *What you did to hurt him or her.*_____

_____

_____

4. *How you think you made this person feel.* _____

_____

_____

5. *Why you are sorry for hurting him or her.*_____

_____

_____

_____

LIFE'S
Healing Choices
AMENDS LIST

1. *His or her name and relationship to you.* _____

_____

_____

2. *What you said to hurt this person.* _____

_____

_____

3. *What you did to hurt him or her.* _____

_____

_____

4. *How you think you made this person feel.* _____

_____

_____

5. *Why you are sorry for hurting him or her.* _____

_____

_____

_____

ACTION 3: *Share about It*

Offering Forgiveness

Go back and review pages 171–75 of *Life's Healing Choices*. It is very important that you share your Forgiveness List with your accountability partner prior to sharing it with the person who hurt you. Your accountability partner can help you develop a plan for safely offering your forgiveness to those on your list. Your accountability partner also knows you and can challenge you to include anyone you may have omitted.

It is vital when offering forgiveness that you do not allow the person to hurt you further. Using your accountability partner as a sounding board will help minimize the risk.

On pages 173–74 of *Life's Healing Choices*, we are given suggestions on ways to offer our forgiveness when it is unwise or not safe to do so face-to-face. Use the empty chair technique with your accountability partner to offer forgiveness when a face-to-face meeting is not safe or appropriate. You can also share your unmailed letter with your accountability partner, when you determine that a letter is the best approach.

How did sharing your Forgiveness List with your accountability partner make you feel?

_____

_____

_____

_____

What plans did you develop for starting to offer your forgiveness to those on your list?

_____

_____

_____

_____

_____

Making Amends

Go back and review pages 177–81 of *Life's Healing Choices*. Be sure to also share your Amends List with your accountability partner. An objective opinion can ensure that you make amends with the right motives. The Bible encourages us to *"consider how we may spur one another on toward love and good deeds"* (Hebrews 10:24 NIV). Just as your accountability partner helped you offer your forgiveness, he or she can help you plan the right time and place to make your amends. For example, if you owe someone money, your accountability partner can help you develop restitution plans.

You need your accountability partner to encourage you to make all the amends on your list. Just as in offering forgiveness, it may not always be safe to make amends face-to-face. Refer to page 179 of *Life's Healing Choices* for more information. Once that is done, there will be no skeletons in your closet. Then you will have come to the point in your life where you can say, "I have nothing more to hide. I'm not perfect, I have attempted to repair all the harmful things I've done in my past. I have made amends and offered restitution for my part."

How did sharing your Amends List with your accountability partner make you feel?

_____

_____

_____

_____

_____

_____

What plans did you develop for starting to offer your amends to those on your list?

_____

_____

_____

_____

_____

_____

_____

CHOICE 6

THE RELATIONSHIP CHOICE

Evaluate all my relationships.

Offer forgiveness to those who have hurt me,
and make amends for harm I've done to others,
except when to do so would harm them or others.

As God frees you from your hurts, hang-ups, and habits, He will reveal significant insights about yourself and others. On these pages, you can keep a daily journal of what God shows you and the progress and growth you are making day by day.

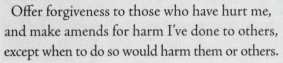

THE RELATIONSHIP CHOICE

Evaluate all my relationships.

Offer forgiveness to those who have hurt me,
and make amends for harm I've done to others,
except when to do so would harm them or others.

_____

_____

_____

_____

_____

_____

_____

_____

_____

_____

_____

_____

_____

_____

_____

_____

_____

_____

"Happy are those who are merciful to others."

Matthew 5:7 TEV

"You must make allowance for each other's faults, and forgive anyone who offends you. Remember, the Lord forgave you, so you must forgive others."
COLOSSIANS 3:13 NLT

_____

_____

_____

_____

_____

_____

_____

_____

_____

_____

_____

_____

_____

_____

_____

_____

_____

_____

_____

_____

_____

_____

_____

_____

_____

_____

_____

_____

_____

_____

_____

THE RELATIONSHIP CHOICE

Evaluate all my relationships.

Offer forgiveness to those who have hurt me,
and make amends for harm I've done to others,
except when to do so would harm them or others.

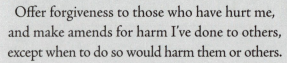

THE RELATIONSHIP CHOICE

Evaluate all my relationships.

Offer forgiveness to those who have hurt me, and make amends for harm I've done to others, except when to do so would harm them or others.

_____

_____

_____

_____

_____

_____

_____

_____

_____

_____

_____

_____

_____

_____

_____

_____

_____

_____

_____

_____

_____

_____

_____

_____

_____

_____

_____

_____

_____

_____

_____

_____

_____

_____

"Happy are those who work for peace."
MATTHEW 5:9 TEV

"Get rid of all bitterness, rage and anger, brawling and slander, along with every form of malice. Be kind and compassionate to one another, forgiving each other, just as in Christ God forgave you."

EPHESIANS 4:31–32 NIV

_____

_____

_____

_____

_____

_____

_____

_____

_____

_____

_____

_____

_____

CHOICE 6

The RELATIONSHIP Choice

Evaluate all my relationships.

Offer forgiveness to those who have hurt me, and make amends for harm I've done to others, except when to do so would harm them or others.

CHOICE 6

The RELATIONSHIP Choice

Evaluate all my relationships.

Offer forgiveness to those who have hurt me,
and make amends for harm I've done to others,
except when to do so would harm them or others.

_____

_____

_____

_____

_____

_____

_____

_____

_____

_____

_____

_____

_____

_____

_____

_____
_____
_____
_____
_____
_____
_____
_____
_____
_____
_____
_____
_____
_____
_____
_____
_____
_____
_____

"You are only hurting yourself with your anger."
JOB 18:4 TEV

*"Let the peace of Christ rule in your hearts, since as members
of one body you were called to peace. And be thankful."*
COLOSSIANS 3:15 NIV

_____

_____

_____

_____

_____

_____

_____

_____

_____

_____

_____

_____

_____

_____

The RELATIONSHIP Choice

Evaluate all my relationships.

Offer forgiveness to those who have hurt me,
and make amends for harm I've done to others,
except when to do so would harm them or others.

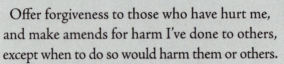

THE RELATIONSHIP CHOICE

Evaluate all my relationships.

Offer forgiveness to those who have hurt me, and make amends for harm I've done to others, except when to do so would harm them or others.

_____

_____

_____

_____

_____

_____

_____

_____

_____

_____

_____

_____

_____

_____

_____

_____

_____

_____

_____

_____

_____

_____

_____

_____

_____

_____

_____

_____

_____

_____

_____

"Look after each other so that not one of you will fail to find God's best blessings. Watch out that no bitterness takes root among you, for as it springs up it causes deep trouble, hurting many in their spiritual lives."

HEBREWS 12:15 TLB

R
E
C
O
V
E
R
Y

Reserve a daily time with God

for self-examination, Bible reading, and prayer

in order *to know* God and His will for my

life and to gain the power to follow His will.

Maintaining MOMENTUM

Make the GROWTH Choice

ACTION 1: *Pray about It*

Praying the Scripture may be another new experience for you, but it's a prayer method that brings amazing blessings. In this action step, we'll pray through the Lord's Prayer (Matthew 6:9–13). You will see how the eight choices support this great prayer. Even though you haven't yet come to Choice 8, you'll be able to pray this choice, too. As we pray, we'll focus our prayer to avoid the dangers of relapse.

> *Scripture: "Our Father in heaven, hallowed be your name . . ."*
> Choice 1: Realize I am not God . . .
> Choice 2: Earnestly believe that God exists . . .
> *Prayer: Father in heaven, Your name is wonderful and holy. I acknowledge that You hold all power—that You are God and that on my own I am powerless. Without You, I will most certainly relapse into my old hurts, hang-ups, and habits.*

Scripture: "Your kingdom come . . ."

Choice 8: Yield myself to God to be used . . .

Prayer: I pray that Your kingdom will come into my life—that I will yield myself to be used by You, that You can use me to reach out to others with the Good News of Your kingdom and Your healing. Help me to find ways to serve You and others.

Scripture: "Your will be done on earth as it is in heaven . . ."

Choice 5: Voluntarily submit to God's changes . . .

Prayer: Oh, Lord, I pray that Your will be done in my life. I fight against it so often, but in my heart of hearts, I choose to submit to You. Help me to hold on to that choice. I choose Your will over my willpower; help me not to fall back into old patterns.

Scripture: "Give us today our daily bread . . ."

Choice 3: Consciously choose to commit . . . to Christ's care . . .

Prayer: Supply me with just what I need for today. Help me to take my recovery one day at a time, not looking too far ahead, but committing all my life and will to Christ's care and control—one day at a time.

Scripture: "Forgive us our debts . . ."

Choice 4: Openly examine and confess my faults . . .

Prayer: Forgive me, Lord. I have looked at my life and my heart, and what I've seen is not pretty. You already knew that, and I thank You for loving me anyway and for forgiving me so freely. Thank You for the loving support from others that You have provided along my healing journey.

Scripture: "As we also have forgiven our debtors . . ."

Choice 6: Evaluate all my relationships . . .

Prayer: Soften my heart toward those who have harmed me. Teach me, by Your power, to forgive, as You have forgiven me. And give me the courage, the conviction, and the wisdom to make amends where I have harmed others. Help me not to relapse into old patterns of resentment and bitterness.

Scripture: "And lead us not into temptation, but deliver us from the evil one . . ."

Choice 7: Reserve a daily time with God . . .

Prayer: Help me to spend time with You daily. I know that time with You is my best defense against relapse and my best offense toward growth. May my time with You create a hedge of protection around me. Amen.

After you have prayed the GROWTH CHOICE prayer, how do you feel? More important, what did God show you about yourself and your actions?

_____

_____

_____

_____

_____

ACTION 2: *Write about It*

One of the habits we talked about in the Preventing Relapse section, on page 213 of *Life's Healing Choices*, is the habit of *evaluation*. Spend some time writing about the four areas discussed there: *physical, emotional, relational,* and *spiritual*. Use these questions to guide your writings.

1. *Physical:* **What is your body telling you? Remember, your body serves as a warning light, alerting you to things that are wrong.**

   _____

   _____

   _____

   _____

   _____

   _____

2. *Emotional:* **What are you feeling? Try to be honest as you write so that you do not repress or stuff your feelings. Use the H-E-A-R-T check to identify what's going on inside of you:**

   H—am I *hurting?*

   E—am I *exhausted?*

   A—am I *angry?*

   R—do I *resent anybody?*

   T—am I *tense?*

_____

_____

_____

_____

_____

_____

_____

_____

3. *Relational:* Am I at peace with everyone? Do I need to make amends to anyone? Do I need to forgive anyone? Write honestly about any conflicts you're having and what your responsibility in the conflict may be so you don't relapse into your old habits.

_____

_____

_____

_____

_____

_____

_____

_____

4. *Spiritual:* Am I relying on God? Take a moment to write about where you are in your relationship with God and what you can do to move your relationship to the next level.

_____

_____

_____

_____

_____

_____

_____

ACTION 3: *Share about It*

Share what you wrote in your "Write about It" section with your accountability partner. You can share with him or her daily if you're going through a tough time. Your accountability partner can help you develop a godly plan to resolve each problem promptly. If you acted out and owe someone amends, share that with your accountability partner, too. This person can help you see your part and pray with you about making your amends.

As you share your evaluation and journal with your accountability partner, ask him or her to help you see any unhealthy patterns that are developing and any old hurts, hang-ups, and habits that are resurfacing.

Review "The Predictable Pattern of Relapse," found on pages 206–208 of *Life's Healing Choices, complacency, confusion, compromise,* and *catastrophe,* with your accountability partner, and ask him or her to help you look honestly at your life to see if any of these patterns are there. Listen openly, and talk together about ways to turn things around and prevent relapses in the future.

What did you learn from sharing your answers in your "Write about It" section with your accountability partner?

_____

_____

_____

_____

_____

Write down any unhealthy patterns that may be developing and any old hurts, hang-ups, and habits that are resurfacing.

_____

_____

_____

_____

_____

_____

What did you learn about reviewing "The Predictable Pattern of Relapse" with your accountability partner?

_____

_____

_____

_____

_____

_____

_____

Congratulations are in order! You have completed seven Life's Healing Choices! You have done a lot of hard work. You admitted that you have a need for help over a hurt, hang-up, or a habit. You also reached out to someone as an accountability partner to get that help. You let go and made the most important commitment of your life by accepting Jesus Christ as your Savior. Then you came clean and faced the truth about your past and present circumstances. With God's help you are working on making some major changes in your life, and you are doing your part in repairing relationships that may have been broken for years. You are now journaling daily and maintaining your momentum by growing closer to God.

Your healing journey took time. It was not completed in days, weeks, or even months. But you are remaining faithful and allowing God to work in your life!

Now, as you begin the eighth choice, you are ready to start recycling your pain! You are ready to start sharing with others the freedom, healing, and victories that God has given you over your hurts, hang-ups, and habits.

THE GROWTH CHOICE

CHOICE 7

Reserve a daily time with God

for self-examination, Bible reading, and prayer in order to know God and His will for my life and to gain the power to follow His will.

As God frees you from your hurts, hang-ups, and habits, He will reveal significant insights about yourself and others. On these pages, you can keep a daily journal of what God shows you and the progress and growth you are making day by day.

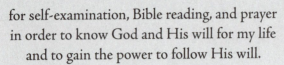

CHOICE 7

The GROWTH Choice

Reserve a daily time with God

for self-examination, Bible reading, and prayer
in order to know God and His will for my life
and to gain the power to follow His will.

_____

_____

_____

_____

_____

_____

_____

_____

_____

_____

_____

_____

_____

"How can you be so foolish! You began by God's Spirit;
do you now want to finish by your own power?"
GALATIANS 3:3 TEV

"You were doing so well! Who made you stop obeying the truth? How did he persuade you?"

Galatians 5:7 TEV

_____

_____

_____

_____

_____

_____

_____

_____

_____

_____

_____

_____

_____

_____

_____

_____

_____

_____

_____

_____

_____

_____

_____

_____

_____

_____

_____

_____

_____

_____

The GROWTH Choice

Reserve a daily time with God

for self-examination, Bible reading, and prayer
in order to know God and His will for my life
and to gain the power to follow His will.

The GROWTH Choice

Reserve a daily time with God

for self-examination, Bible reading, and prayer
in order to know God and His will for my life
and to gain the power to follow His will.

_____

_____

_____

_____

_____

_____

_____

_____

_____

_____

_____

_____

_____

_____

_____

_____

_____

_____

_____

_____

_____

_____

_____

_____

_____

_____

_____

_____

_____

_____

_____

_____

_____

_____

"Pride goes before destruction and haughtiness before a fall."
PROVERBS 16:18 TLB

"Humble yourselves before the Lord, and he will lift you up."

JAMES 4:10 NIV

_____

_____

_____

_____

_____

_____

_____

_____

_____

_____

_____

_____

_____

CHOICE 7

The GROWTH Choice

Reserve a daily time with God

for self-examination, Bible reading, and prayer
in order to know God and His will for my life
and to gain the power to follow His will.

THE GROWTH CHOICE

Reserve a daily time with God

for self-examination, Bible reading, and prayer
in order to know God and His will for my life
and to gain the power to follow His will.

_____

_____

_____

_____

_____

_____

_____

_____

_____

_____

_____

_____

_____

_____

_____

_____

_____

_____

_____

_____

_____

_____

_____

_____

_____

_____

_____

_____

_____

_____

_____

"Watch and pray so that you will not fall into temptation.
The spirit is willing, but the body is weak."

Mark 14:38 NIV

"Test yourselves to make sure you are solid in the faith. Don't drift along taking everything for granted. Give yourselves regular checkups. You need firsthand evidence, not mere hearsay, that Jesus Christ is in you. Test it out. If you fail the test, do something about it."

2 Corinthians 13:5 MSG

_____

_____

_____

_____

_____

_____

_____

_____

_____

_____

_____

_____

THE GROWTH CHOICE

Reserve a daily time with God

for self-examination, Bible reading, and prayer
in order to know God and His will for my life
and to gain the power to follow His will.

THE GROWTH CHOICE

Reserve a daily time with God

for self-examination, Bible reading, and prayer
in order to know God and His will for my life
and to gain the power to follow His will.

_____

_____

_____

_____

_____

_____

_____

_____

_____

_____

_____

_____

_____

_____

*"Let's take a good look at the way we're living
and reorder our lives under God."*

LAMENTATIONS 3:40 MSG

R
E
C
O
V
E
R

"Happy are those who are persecuted
because they do what God requires."
Matthew 5:10 TEV

Yield myself to God

to be *used* to bring this Good News to others,

both by my example and by my words.

Recycling PAIN

Make the SHARING Choice

ACTION 1: *Pray about It*

Ask God to lead you to somebody to share your story with, the Good News of how God made a difference in your life and how He can make the difference in theirs.

You can begin each day with a prayer something like this:

Dear God, help me to be ready to share with someone today the victories You have given me. Help me find the right words and the right time to share my heart with someone who is hurting and doesn't know where to go or how to stop the pain. I pray that I can share the ways you freed me from my hurts, hang-ups, and habits. Let me do so with gentleness and respect. Thank You for letting me serve You today in this way. Amen.

After you prayed the SHARING CHOICE prayer, how do you feel? More important, what did God show you about yourself and your actions?

_____

_____

_____

_____

_____

_____

_____

_____

Did God show you a person who needs to hear your story?

_____

_____

_____

_____

_____

ACTION 2: *Write about It*

If you prayed the prayer in the first action step, you need to prepare in advance to share your story. How do you get prepared to share your story? Review the three guidelines found on pages 249–50 of *Life's Healing Choices*, under the heading "Tell Your Story." The following are some suggestions to help you get started.

+ **Make a brief list of all the experiences that have significantly impacted your life to this day—positive and negative. Write down the ones you caused and the ones you didn't. Look back at your Moral Inventory on pages 78–81 of your journal. It will help you remember these experiences.**

_____

_____

_____

_____

_____

_____

_____

_____

_____

_____

_____

_____

+ Next, write out what you learned from each experience.

_____

_____

_____

_____

_____

_____

_____

_____

_____

_____

_____

_____

_____

_____

_____

_____

+ Write about how God helped you make it through the tough times.

_____

_____

_____

_____

_____

_____

_____

_____

+ Make a list of the people who need to hear your story.

_____

_____

_____

_____

_____

_____

+ Write your story.

Why is it so important to write out your story? Remember, thoughts disentangle themselves when they pass through the lips to the fingertips. Write it out.

My Story

My Story

My Story

ACTION 3: *Share about It*

After you have written out your story, your testimony, share it with your accountability partner. He or she can serve as a good sounding board. Your accountability partner has been with you from the start of your healing journey and knows you and your story. Your partner can help you review your story and ensure that you haven't left out any important events that would be helpful to others. They can also help you share your story in a way that is humble, real, and not lecturing.

How did you feel after you shared your story with your accountability partner?

_____

_____

_____

_____

_____

_____

What changes did they suggest you make?

_____

_____

_____

_____

_____

_____

_____

_____

_____

_____

_____

_____

_____

Make the changes that you believe are necessary and start sharing your story.

Tell God you're available and then get ready. If you are prepared to share the Good News of how God has worked in your life, God will wear you out.

Can you imagine getting to heaven and someone saying to you, "I'm in heaven because of you, and I just want to thank you"? Do you think that sharing your story will have been worth it? It will far outlast anything you do in your career, anything you do in your hobby. We're talking about *eternal* implications—getting people from darkness into light, from hell into heaven, from an eternity without God to an eternity with God. People will be thanking you for the rest of eternity. There is nothing more significant in life.

—*Life's Healing Choices*, page 250

IMPORTANT NOTE: Another way you can continue to live out Choice 8, the SHARING Choice, is to start a Life's Healing Choices Small Group! In your group, you can help others go through the book, *Life's Healing Choices*, so they can begin their own healing journey of finding freedom from their lives' hurts, hang-ups, and habits. You can invite your friends, neighbors, and/or coworkers to join. If you are already in a small group at your church, you can suggest they consider using *Life's Healing Choices Small Group Study* curriculum for their next eight-week study.

CHOICE 8

THE SHARING CHOICE
Yield myself to God
to be used to bring this Good News to others, both by my example and by my words.

As God frees you from your hurts, hang-ups, and habits, He will reveal significant insights about yourself and others. On these pages, you can keep a daily journal of what God shows you and the progress and growth you are making day by day.

"Happy are those who are persecuted because they do what God requires."

MATTHEW 5:10 TEV

_____

_____

_____

_____

_____

_____

_____

_____

_____

_____

_____

_____

_____

_____

_____

_____

_____

The SHARING Choice

Yield myself to God

to be used to bring this Good News to others,
both by my example and by my words.

CHOICE 8

_____

_____

_____

_____

_____

_____

_____

_____

_____

_____

_____

_____

_____

_____

_____

_____

_____

_____

_____

_____

_____

_____

_____

_____

_____

_____

_____

_____

"Each time he said, 'My grace is all you need. My power works best in weakness.' So now I am glad to boast about my weaknesses, so that the power of Christ can work through me."
2 Corinthians 12:9 NLT

"Sometimes it takes a painful experience to make us change our ways."

PROVERBS 20:30 TEV

_____

_____

_____

_____

_____

_____

_____

_____

_____

_____

_____

_____

_____

_____

_____

_____

_____

_____

_____

_____

_____

_____

_____

_____

_____

_____

_____

_____

_____

CHOICE 8

THE SHARING CHOICE

Yield myself to God

to be used to bring this Good News to others,
both by my example and by my words.

The SHARING Choice

Yield myself to God

to be used to bring this Good News to others,
both by my example and by my words.

_____

_____

_____

_____

_____

_____

_____

_____

_____

_____

_____

_____

_____

"When I had lost all hope, I turned my thoughts to the Lord.
And my earnest prayer went out to you in your holy Temple."
Jonah 2:7 NLT

199

"I think you ought to know, dear brothers, about the hard time we went through in Asia. We were really crushed and overwhelmed, and feared we would never live through it. We felt we were doomed to die and saw how powerless we were to help ourselves; but that was good, for then we put everything into the hands of God, who alone could save us, for he can even raise the dead."

2 Corinthians 1:8–9 TLB

_____

_____

_____

_____

_____

_____

_____

_____

_____

_____

_____

_____

_____

_____

_____

_____

_____

_____

_____

_____

_____

_____

_____

_____

_____

_____

THE SHARING CHOICE
Yield myself to God
to be used to bring this Good News to others,
both by my example and by my words.

The SHARING Choice

Yield myself to God

to be used to bring this Good News to others,
both by my example and by my words.

_____

_____

_____

_____

_____

_____

_____

_____

_____

_____

_____

_____

_____

_____

_____

_____

_____

_____

_____

_____

_____

_____

_____

_____

_____

_____

_____

_____

_____

_____

*"The suffering you sent was good for me, for it taught
me to pay attention to your principles."*

PSALM 119:71 NLT

"In your hearts set apart Christ as Lord. Always be prepared to give an answer to everyone who asks you to give the reason for the hope that you have. But do this with gentleness and respect."
1 Peter 3:15 NIV

_____

_____

_____

_____

_____

_____

_____

_____

_____

_____

_____

_____

THE SHARING CHOICE
Yield myself to God
to be used to bring this Good News to others,
both by my example and by my words.

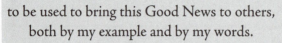

The SHARING Choice
Yield myself to God
to be used to bring this Good News to others,
both by my example and by my words.

CHOICE 8

_____

_____

_____

_____

_____

_____

_____

_____

_____

_____

_____

_____

_____

_____

_____

_____

_____

_____

_____

_____

_____

_____

_____

_____

_____

_____

_____

*"If we confess our sins, he is faithful and just and will forgive
us our sins and purify us from all unrighteousness."*
1 JOHN 1:9 NIV

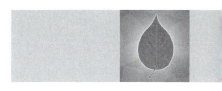

LIFE'S
Healing Choices
PRAYER JOURNAL

"Do not be anxious about anything, but in everything,
by prayer and petition, with thanksgiving,
present your requests to God. And the peace of God,
which transcends all understanding, will
guard your hearts and your minds in Christ Jesus."

PHILIPPIANS 4:6–7 NIV

LIFE'S *Healing Choices* PRAYER JOURNAL

Date Prayed: _____

Prayer Request (be specific): _____

_____

_____

_____

_____

_____

Date Answered: _____

God's Answer (be specific): _____

_____

_____

_____

_____

_____

_____

Date Prayed: _____

Prayer Request (be specific): _____

_____

_____

_____

_____

_____

Date Answered: _____

God's Answer (be specific): _____

_____

_____

_____

_____

_____

"Do not be anxious about anything, but in everything, by prayer and petition, with thanksgiving, present your requests to God. And the peace of God, which transcends all understanding, will guard your hearts and your minds in Christ Jesus."
PHILIPPIANS 4:6–7 NIV

Date Prayed: _____

Prayer Request (be specific): _____

_____

_____

_____

_____

_____

_____

_____

Date Answered: _____

God's Answer (be specific): _____

_____

_____

_____

_____

_____

_____

_____

_____

_____

Date Prayed: _____

Prayer Request (be specific): _____

_____

_____

_____

_____

_____

Date Answered: _____

God's Answer (be specific): _____

_____

_____

_____

_____

_____

"*Do not be anxious about anything, but in everything, by prayer and petition, with thanksgiving, present your requests to God. And the peace of God, which transcends all understanding, will guard your hearts and your minds in Christ Jesus.*"

PHILIPPIANS 4:6–7 NIV

Date Prayed: _____

Prayer Request (be specific): _____

_____

_____

_____

_____

_____

_____

Date Answered: _____

God's Answer (be specific): _____

_____

_____

_____

_____

_____

_____

_____

Date Prayed: _____

Prayer Request (be specific): _____

_____

_____

_____

_____

_____

_____

Date Answered: _____

God's Answer (be specific): _____

_____

_____

_____

_____

_____

"Do not be anxious about anything, but in everything, by prayer and petition, with thanksgiving, present your requests to God. And the peace of God, which transcends all understanding, will guard your hearts and your minds in Christ Jesus."

PHILIPPIANS 4:6–7 NIV

Date Prayed: _____

Prayer Request (be specific): _____

_____

_____

_____

_____

_____

_____

_____

Date Answered: _____

God's Answer (be specific): _____

_____

_____

_____

_____

_____

_____

_____

_____

Date Prayed: _____

Prayer Request (be specific): _____

_____

_____

_____

_____

_____

Date Answered: _____

God's Answer (be specific): _____

_____

_____

_____

_____

_____

"Do not be anxious about anything, but in everything, by prayer and petition, with thanksgiving, present your requests to God. And the peace of God, which transcends all understanding, will guard your hearts and your minds in Christ Jesus."

PHILIPPIANS 4:6–7 NIV

Also Available by John Baker

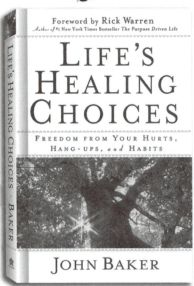

Foreword by Rick Warren
Author of #1 New York Times Bestseller The Purpose Driven Life

LIFE'S HEALING CHOICES

FREEDOM FROM YOUR HURTS,
HANG-UPS, and HABITS

JOHN BAKER

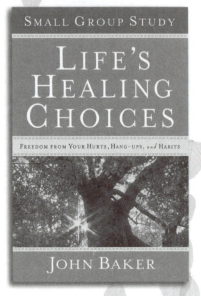

SMALL GROUP STUDY

LIFE'S HEALING CHOICES

FREEDOM FROM YOUR HURTS, HANG-UPS, and HABITS

JOHN BAKER

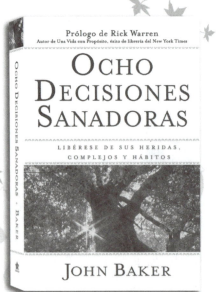

Prólogo de Rick Warren
Autor de Una Vida con Propósito, éxito de librería del New York Times

OCHO DECISIONES SANADORAS

LIBÉRESE DE SUS HERIDAS,
COMPLEJOS Y HÁBITOS

JOHN BAKER

Life's Healing Choices (Spanish)

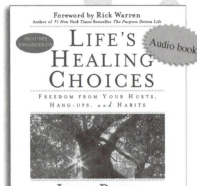

INCLUDES ENHANCED CD

Foreword by Rick Warren
Author of #1 New York Times Bestseller The Purpose Driven Life

LIFE'S HEALING CHOICES

FREEDOM FROM YOUR HURTS,
HANG-UPS, and HABITS

Audio book

JOHN BAKER
Read by the author

HOWARD BOOKS
A DIVISION OF SIMON & SCHUSTER